Dinosaurs
And other poems

Edward Barnes & Brianna Benji

Edward Barnes

Copyright © 2018 BCB Productions

All rights reserved.

ISBN-10:4527893009
ISBN-13:9784527893000

DINOSAURS & other poems

∧∧∧∧∧∧∧∧∧

Edward Barnes

CONTENTS

1	Dinosaurs	1
2	Village of love	Pg
3	The robot	Pg

Edward Barnes

Dinosaurs

came an ice age through all fossils and crust.

Somehow no-one agrees just why,
these reptiles were meant to die.

Wondering when
our time will come,

Village of Love

Skies of blue and possibilities redeem

Might beware the treasures that appear,

This bridge of nature who's one to succeed.

followed by villagers they hunt for their feed.

The Robot

By undesired operation the robot did not understand,

There was move-
ments, this life with
mechanical parts,

Smiles, frowns,
sadness, and tears
winding the gears of
hearts.

There was
no room for
explaining the
need for life
in years,

We started off as pieces a human picture in the mind,

Designed on paper and pencil... shavings left behind.

Meet the authors

Edward Barnes

Edward Barnes and Brianna Benji are both authors and are really good friends. They are also founders of BCB Productions, a small publishing company that hires people with special needs that have creative writing talents of any kind or genre. For more information on BCB PRODUCTIONS visit their website,
www.bcbproductions.weebly.com

www.ingramcontent.com/pod-product-compliance
Lightning Source LLC
Chambersburg PA
CBHW042121040426
42449CB00003B/132